The Australian Outback

Donna Bailey and Jean Chapman

MACMILLAN EDUCATION

Much of the south and middle of Australia
is very hot and dry.
Australians call it the 'Outback'.
The biggest town in the Outback is
Alice Springs which is almost
in the centre of Australia.

Most of the roads in the Outback
don't have any fences, so wild animals
wander across them.
There are lots of kangaroos and emus here.
You can even see herds of wild camels.

The cars have 'roo' bars in front
of their engines.
These are to protect the engines and lights
if kangaroos hop into the road.
Kangaroos often get hit by cars on the roads.

Many of the cars and trucks have shields
over their windscreens.
These stop the stones which flick up
from breaking the windscreens.

Very large trucks called road trains
are used to move goods and cattle
from Alice Springs to the cities.
Road trains often travel together
across the Outback.

Children living in the Outback
don't go to school like other children.
They get their lessons through the post
once a fortnight.
They switch on a special two-way radio at home.
A teacher talks to them over the radio and
they can talk back to the teacher.

People in the Outback use the radio
to talk to each other.
They can warn each other if they need help,
or say where the kangaroos
have broken down their fences.

They also use the radio to call up
the 'Flying Doctor' service.
The doctor talks over the radio and
says what should be done for the patient.
Sometimes the doctor flies in to take
the sick person to hospital.

My uncle has a sheep station in the Outback.
He has thousands of sheep on his station.
His stockmen work with dogs to find the sheep.
They often ride motorbikes to round them up.

When the sheep have all been rounded up,
shearers come and cut off their wool.
The men pack the wool into big bales.
They load the bales into trucks which
take the wool to be sold in the cities.

Some of the stockmen on my uncle's station
are Aborigines.
Aborigines have lived in Australia
for thousands of years.
Some of them work in the Outback and
have their own cattle stations.

Ayer's Rock near Alice Springs
belongs to the Aborigines.
The Aborigines' name for Ayer's Rock is Uluru.
The cave paintings done by Aborigines in
the caves at Uluru are very famous.

There are lots of caves at Uluru.
Long ago the Aborigines made paintings
and drawings on cave walls in many
different places in Australia.

Many of these paintings are sacred.
Others show how the Aborigines live and
how they feel about the land.
Aborigines also have many stories, dances and
songs about the animals and land in the Outback.

Index